The Amazing Mumford Presents
ALL ABOUT BONES

by Jocelyn Stevenson • Illustrated by Normand Chartier

Featuring Jim Henson's Sesame Street Muppets

A SESAME STREET / GOLDEN PRESS BOOK
Published by Western Publishing Company, Inc.
in conjunction with Children's Television Workshop.

© 1980 Children's Television Workshop. The Amazing Mumford and other Muppet
characters © 1980 Muppets, Inc. All rights reserved. Printed in U.S.A. SESAME STREET®,
the SESAME STREET SIGN, and SESAME STREET BOOK CLUB are trademarks
and service marks of Children's Television Workshop. GOLDEN® and GOLDEN PRESS®
are trademarks of Western Publishing Company, Inc. No part of this book
may be reproduced or copied in any form without written permission from the publisher.
Library of Congress Catalog Card Number: 80-68268   ISBN 0-307-23126-7

"Welcome, welcome!" cried the Amazing Mumford. "Today my super-duper magic show is all about bones!" Mumford tapped his magic hat.

"A LA PEANUT BUTTER SANDWICHES!" he said, pulling something out of his hat. "This, my friends, is a bone. Everybody has bones."

POOF!

"Now for my next trick," said Mumfie.
"A LA PEANUT BUTTER SANDWICHES!" And he
pulled a rabbit out of his hat. "My bunny friend here
will assist me. Notice the shape of his body. His bones
give his body its shape!"

Mumford twirled his hat. "All your bones put together make your skeleton! Observe. A LA PEANUT BUTTER SANDWICHES!"
Suddenly a big pile of bones appeared.
"Here we have dinosaur bones."

"With the magic wave of my wand you will see that all these bones put together make a dinosaur skeleton!"

"Yay! Three cheers for Mumfie!" the audience yelled.

"Now," said Mumford, "are there any questions?"
"Yes," answered a little girl named Ginger. She came up on stage. "This is all very interesting, but how do I know I have bones?"

"So glad you asked," said the Amazing Mumford. "Squeeze your finger. That hard thing you feel inside it is a bone!"

Ginger pinched her finger. "Oh, yes," she said, "I can feel something hard."

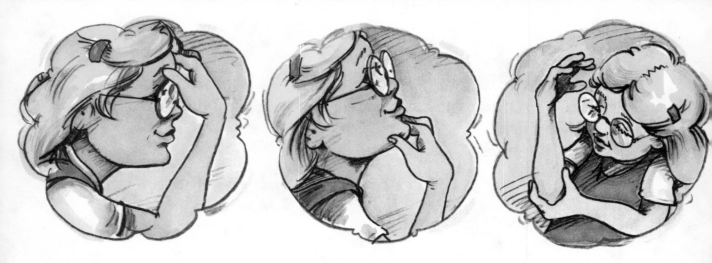

"Now, my little friend," said Mumford, "grab your forehead, your chin, your elbow, your heel, your ankle, and your knees!"

"I can feel my bones!" said Ginger.

"Yes!" cried Mumford.

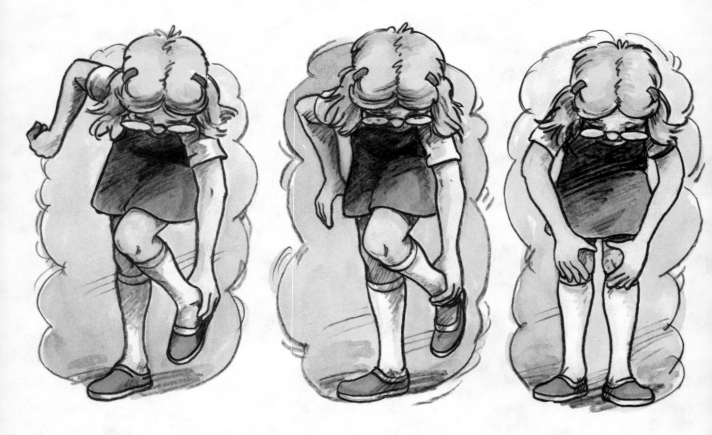

"I have another question, Mr. Mumford," said Ginger.

"Proceed."

"Well, you said all my bones put together make my skeleton," she said.

"Right again," said Mumford.

"My question is—what does my skeleton look like?"

"Excellent question, my clever friend," said Mumford.
"Watch carefully." Mumford closed his eyes and held his magic hat
in his hands. "A LA PEANUT BUTTER SANDWICHES!" he yelled.

And the Amazing Mumford pulled a picture of a skeleton
out of his hat. "This is what your skeleton looks like.
Notice the lovely bones in the tail."

"But, Mr. Mumford," said Ginger, "I don't have a tail."

"No, but I do," barked a dog in the audience. "That must be a picture of what my skeleton looks like." The dog jumped up on stage and stood next to the picture.

"Hmmm...right you are, sir. Right you are," said Mumfie. He gave the picture to the dog. Mumfie looked at Ginger. "If at first you don't succeed...."

"A LA PEANUT BUTTER SANDWICHES!" he cried.
And he pulled another skeleton picture out of his hat.
    "There you are," said Mumford proudly to Ginger.
"What lovely flippers you have!"
    "Wait a minute!" said a seal in the audience.
"She doesn't have flippers—I do."
    The seal waddled up on stage and studied the picture.

"Look," she said. "That's a seal skeleton if I ever saw one." And she waddled off the stage with the picture. "Oh, dear," said Mumford, "wrong again."

"A LA PEANUT BUTTER SANDWICHES!"

"Ah ha!" said Mumford, looking at the picture that appeared in his hand. "This is what your skeleton looks like, Ginger. I never knew you had such a nice, long back!"

"I don't," said Ginger.

"But I do," hissed a snake. She slithered on stage and lay next to the skeleton picture. "Assss you can sssssee, that issss my ssssssskeleton, ssssir," said the snake. "And it'ssss gorgeousss, if I do ssssay sssso mysssssself."

"Yes," said Mumfie sadly. "I ssssee what you mean."

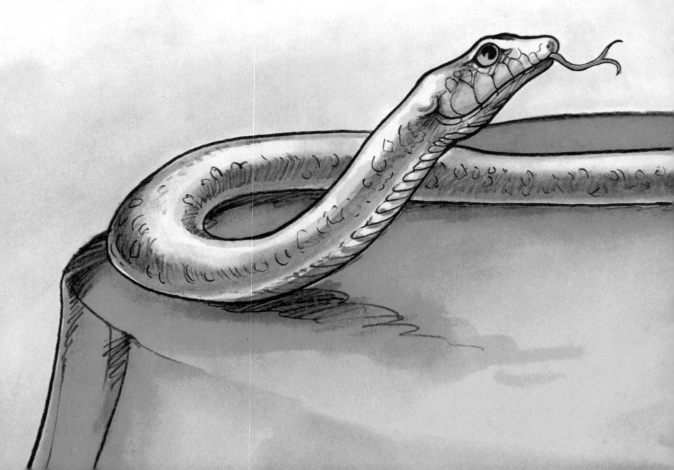

Mumford scratched his head. He stared at his hat.
"A LA PEANUT BUTTER SANDWICHES!" he shrieked.
And out of the hat popped another picture of a skeleton.

Mumfie looked at the picture. Then he looked at Ginger.
"I don't suppose you have wings?" he asked hopefully.

"Of course not," said Ginger. "That isn't my skeleton."

"It must be mine!" chirped a beautiful bird.
He flew up to the stage and looked at the picture.
  "Yes, that's mine all right. It will look wonderful
above my nest." He picked up the picture and flew
off with it.

Ginger was getting impatient. "What about my skeleton?" she asked.

"It's coming!" said Mumford.

"A LA PEANUT BUTTER SANDWICHES!" He pulled a newspaper out of his hat.

Mumfie opened the paper. "There you are! I told you! A marvelous skeleton!" he cried.

"Thank you very much," neighed a horse sitting in the audience. She loped on stage. "That belongs to me, as you can see. This girl doesn't have four legs, but I do."

"A LA PEANUT BUTTER SANDWICHES!" Mumford sighed wearily. This time he pulled out a piece of paper all rolled up.

Mumford unrolled and unrolled the long roll of paper. He looked at the picture. He looked at Ginger. He looked back at the picture.

"Wrong again," he said. "Is there by any chance a giraffe in the audience?"

"Why, yes!" said a giraffe, waking from a short nap. "Oh, look! You've got a picture of my skeleton!"

The giraffe walked on stage
and stood next to the picture.
   "Yes, that's my lovely long neck!"
he said, and he trotted off the stage
with the picture.

"I'll try one more time," said Mumford. He placed his hands very carefully on his magic hat. He took a deep breath. "A LA PEANUT BUTTER SANDWICHES!" he said slowly.

Mumford looked at the picture he had pulled from his hat, and started to cry.

"Oh no!" he wailed. "I've failed again!"

"Wait a minute," said Ginger. "You've got it upside down."

Mumford turned the picture right side up.

"Look," Ginger said. "This skeleton has two arms. I have two arms. This skeleton has two legs. I have two legs. This is a picture of my skeleton! Mr. Mumford, you've done it!"

Everybody in the audience stood up and cheered.

"Hooray for Mumfie!"

"Of course I've done it!" said Mumford. "Did you think that I wouldn't?"

"Oh, no, Mr. Mumford. I knew you could do it," said Ginger. "But I have one more little favor to ask you."

"Anything you want, Ginger!"

With that, Ginger whistled, and the hugest, weirdest, most lovable monster in the world lumbered up on the stage.

"This is my best friend, Flo," said Ginger. "Now, Mr. Mumford, sir, can you please show us what her skeleton looks like?"

But the Amazing Mumford was too amazed to try.

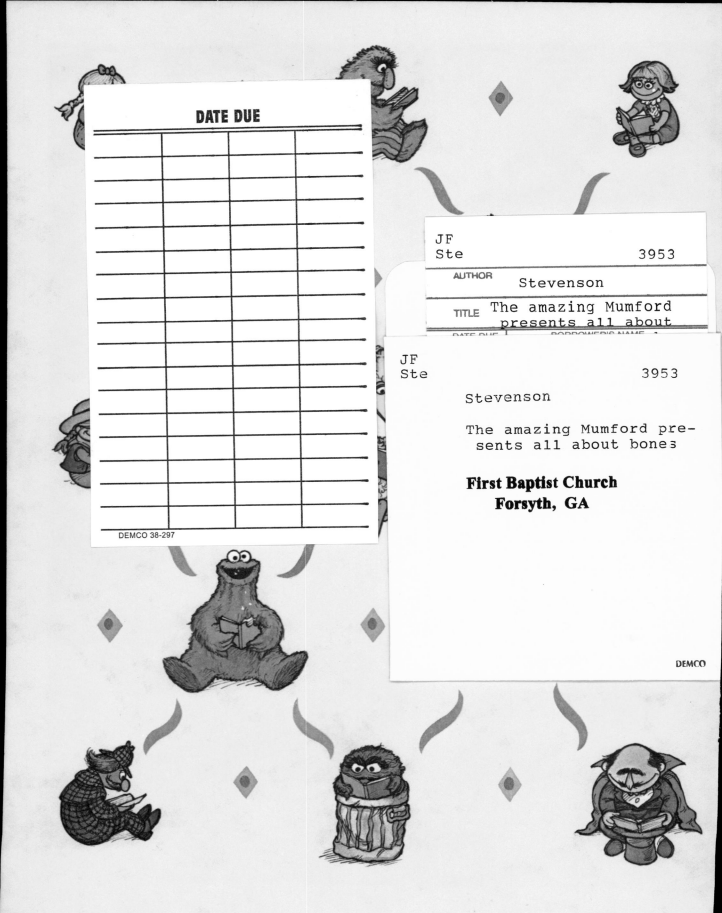

DATE DUE

DEMCO 38-297

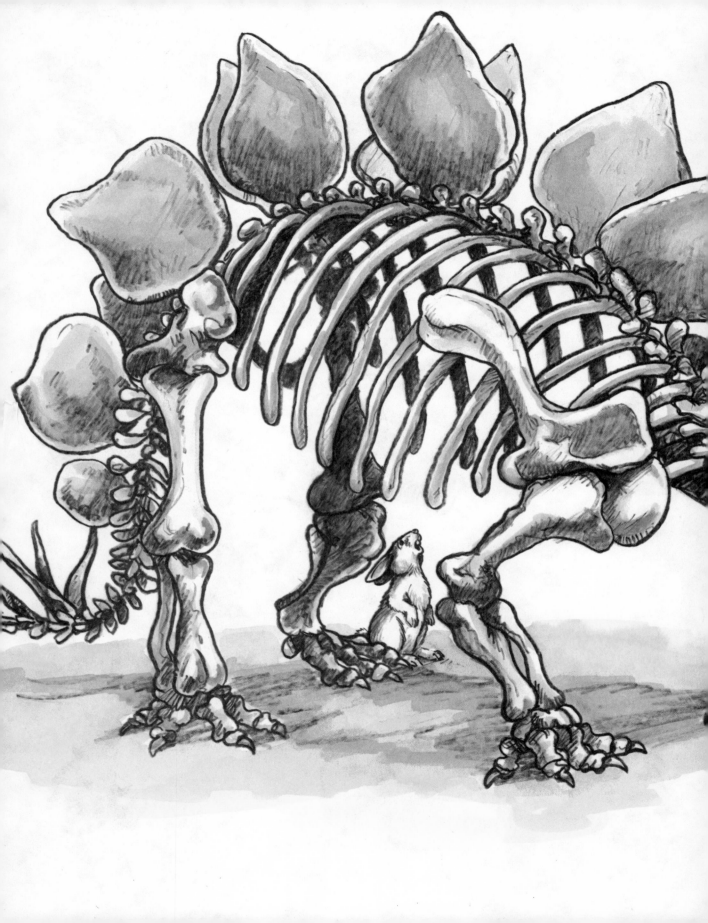